Praise
Poems for Soulful Living

*Thank you for your poems, they are very soul nourishing,
particularly at this time.*
—Jane

*The poem you wrote about resting was beautiful. I was reading it in
tears. I could just feel loads of relaxing and calming vibes filling my
body while reading it. It was truly so lovely.*
—Jacquelin

Beautiful wisdom, I'm taking it in.
—Lysa

*This was such a beautiful and powerful practice, Nadege. Thank
you so much for your guidance, encouragement and lovely
supportive words and presence. I feel like it really helped my
transformation of fully letting go and moving forward because it
enabled me to envision how things could be. Thank you for your
wisdom, it is exactly what I needed!*
—Annabel

Mmm, so good!
—Amy

*I love this, beautiful Nadege, I will share it, so many
people need to hear it.*
—Angela

It is as if you were painting my body with your words.
—Anita

POEMS
for
SOULFUL
LIVING

POEMS
for
SOULFUL
LIVING

*

NADEGE LAURE

A catalogue record for this book is available from the National Library of Australia.

Trade Paperback ISBN: 978-0-6458993-0-6
eBook ISBN: 978-0-6458993-1-3

Print information available on the last page.

We at The Kind Press acknowledge that Aboriginal and Torres Strait Islander peoples are the Traditional Custodians and the first storytellers of the lands on which we live and work; and we pay our respects to Elders past and present.

THE
KIND
PRESS

www.thekindpress.com

To my mum, for everything she was and taught me,
and for showing me how to embrace life.

While you sip on a cup of tea...

CONTENTS

.

DEAR ONE

Dear one,
Once you embark on the journey to find yourself, you will no longer be restricted.
Once you open the door onto your quest for answers and meaning, there is no turning back.
Once you start searching for your truth and inherent purpose, you won't be able to stop or dismiss what you find.
Once you take a step towards your dharma, your true calling, you cannot ignore it or let it go.

With all your heart,
with all your mind,
with your whole being,
you will follow this strong impulse and unspeakable drive onto your journey of self-discovery.

This is why we are here.
This is what we are meant to be doing:
Soulful living.

INVOCATION

I open my heart
To the wisdom and guidance
That bring the unfolding of
My truest transformation

POEMS *for* SOULFUL LIVING

How beautiful it is to do nothing and rest afterwards.

—Spanish proverb

REST

Recline
Rest your head, darling

Close your eyes
Feel your breath

Rest
Do nothing

It is not a luxury
It is a necessity

It is not a reward or a treat
but the deepest act of self-care

Rest
Do nothing

There's nothing to lose and so much to gain
More space, ease, inspiration and creativity

Gift yourself this interval of non-doing
A time to recharge, to day dream, to be

Just for a moment
Cease all activities

Rest
Do nothing

There's virtue in discipline and work,
There's also virtue in rest

Rest
Do nothing
Take your time

We are living in a culture entirely hypnotized by the illusion of time, in which the so-called present moment is felt as nothing but an infinitesimal hairline between an all-powerfully causative past and an absorbingly important future. We have no present. Our consciousness is almost completely preoccupied with memory and expectation. We do not realize that there never was, is, nor will be any other experience than present experience. We are therefore out of touch with reality. We confuse the world as talked about, described, and measured with the world which actually is.

—Alan W. Watts

STILLNESS

Pause.
Become still.
Breathe.
The breath.
Your breath.
Its rhythm. Its sound. Its texture. Its depth. Its teaching.
This moment.
This breath.
The present.

Find stillness.
In stillness, meet your Self.
In stillness, breathe together.
This moment.
This breath.
The present.
In stillness, the universe surrenders.
Stillness. Silence. Breath.

A sacred moment.
For yourself, with yourself.
Accessing the innermost, wisest truth of your entire being.
The essence of your soul.
This moment.
This breath.

In stillness, opening the doorway to your soul.
In stillness, paying attention to its murmur
In stillness, finding home.

Be a light unto yourself; betake yourselves to no external refuge. Hold fast to the Truth. Look not for refuge to anyone besides yourselves.

—Buddha Shakyamuni

YOU KNOW

YOU are stronger than you think.

You are a catalyst.

You unconsciously know your strength and what you truly want.

You have everything you need within you.

You sense what is right for you to do.

Dive within.

Peel the layers through self-study.

Listen to your inner wisdom for that your truth resides inside your heart.

Deep inside you KNOW.

Open up to the instinctive knowing,

Your intuition.

Trust it and follow it.

It will not lead you astray.

And shine your own beautiful, bright, unique light.

We need you,

You know.

SIMPLY BEING

Quietude
Mother Nature
The breeze caressing me
The sound of the waves lulling me
Breathing it all in
Nourishing my mind, my body and my soul
Finding stillness
Discovering peace
In simply being

GO FORWARD FEARLESSLY

Into the unknown
Into uncertainty
Out of your comfort zone
In the light or in the dark
Regardless of what is in store,
Go forward fearlessly.

If you feel tingling in your solar plexus,
Go forward fearlessly
If you don't know what to do, believe in your inkling and
Go forward fearlessly
If it means saying no to situations or people that keep you
small,
Go forward fearlessly
If it is aligned with your profound wisdom,
Go forward fearlessly.

Go forward fearlessly
Knowing that you are supported,
Smiling at the abundance of unexpected possibilities,
Discovering your inner strength
Yes, indeed, go forward fearlessly for you are honouring your
sacredness.
Acknowledge the wisdom of your heart and soul,
Go forward fearlessly

Don't be less than what you are.

Go forward fearlessly
For that is the key to happiness.

AT NIGHT

Sometimes
When I stay up at night
In the mesmerising quiet and hypnotic beauty
I can hear the cries for help from all the suffering souls
I feel the exhaustion of the breastfeeding moms
I feel the frightened one running for her life
I feel the gloom, the doom and alarm of the city
This one and others
The refugee camps
I empathise with the less fortunate
And wonder why them, not me?
And I look out the window
Closer
I see the lights
I remember than only in the darkness we can see the stars
I watch outside, motionless
The mesmerising quiet and hypnotic beauty
Fills me with hope
When I stay up at night
Reminisce, create and hear the voices past
I look up at the starry sky
And smile admiringly
For this day
For this night
For this life so far

When you just sit in silence the wind blows through you,
the sun shines in you, and you realize you are not your body;
you are everything.

—Anita Krizzan

SILENCE

They say it is heavy
Uncomfortable
Deafening
Gnawing
Dead

They say that speech is silver, but silence is gold
A few silences have told me a thousand words
Some have left me lost and worried
Others soothed me and rejuvenated me

Sometimes silence is so loud
It penetrates me
I soak in it
And I can hear my interior world

Forbidden to speak for ten days
Was one of the most telling experiences of my life
Every time
I could hear it all:
The wind, the plants, the sun,
My heartbeat and blood pumping,
Myself

Was this sonic isolation a hallucinatory symphony?
Was Life speaking to me?
My thoughts were blaring, my understandings resounding
Forbearing withholding my spoken word

I humbly received the gifts of escaping the pandemonium of
the world

I rejoiced in obmutescence
And the silence of the calm open sea delivered its subtleties

A WINTER NIGHT

As we plant the seed in the bare, cold soil
It lies dormant for months
Of withdrawing, resting and reflecting

The most yin time of year
Lightless, motionless
Yet the river keeps flowing silently along the snowy field

Cold outside, snug inside
Introspection
We welcome the slowing down and hibernation

A time to journal, meditate, knit and sip tea
Contemplation
A time to watch the snow fall out the window

Reverie
Wondering when the darkest night will end
And if the light and warmth will ever come again

ON THE JOURNEY TO OPEN HEART

Open your heart and breathe deeply
Even if you can't see what is there
Even if you don't know what is coming

Open your heart and dwell in possibilities
Hopeful and trusting
Calm and resolute

Open your heart to create space in your body
To fill it with love, elation and contentment
You and only you choose what enters that space

Open your heart and
Allow love to overflow
Grant this nourishment to your soul
Recognise the uplift of Spirit

Open your heart and let ebullience fly in
Let it sweep you off your feet
Then follow the thrill like stardust

On the journey to open heart
Expand your heart
For when the heart opens,
The mind follows

Slowly, as we surrender to the openness
We start moving from the head to the heart
From thinking to being
From fearing to trusting
From doubting to knowing

Open your heart
For all your wisdom lies there
The heart always knows the way

It is our best teacher

WHAT IF

What if you are not your sadness, your grief, your anxiety?
What if you are not your doubts and indecisions?
What if you are not your worries or the nagging voice
within?
What if you are not others' perception of you?
Well, my beautiful friend, you aren't

So, what if you let go of restraints, rules, dogma, beliefs?
What if you removed all fences between you and Love?
What if you constantly showered yourself with gentle, tender,
loving care?
What would happen then?

What if you forgave yourself?
What if you embraced all of your idiosyncrasies?
What if you honoured your needs?
What if you gave yourself permission to candidly be you?
To simply do what feels true and what you really want to do?

What if you allowed yourself to feel confident?
What if you tapped into your inner power?
What if you disregarded the box and labels that are reducing
your capabilities?
What if you were unapologetically your unique, radiant Self?

What if you just bloomed?
What would happen then?

A CACAO PRAYER

With this cup of cacao,
I let myself receive the healing and yearning energy of this
new moon
I allow my exhale to remove any tension and obstacle
I let the plant lovingly nourish and soothe me.

With this cup of cacao,
I acknowledge and honour every aspect of myself:
My light and my shadow
My strengths and my weaknesses
My yin and my yang
My past wounds and my future self
My courage for saying no and reclaiming my freedom
My choice to only proceed with whatever feels delightful.
I open to my heart leading the way
I listen to my soul whispering to me
I bow to my power revealing itself.

With this cup of cacao,
I quit avoiding my purpose and I wholeheartedly dive in
The spirit of the plant fills me up
It supports me in standing strong,
Uncovering my potential,
And in occupying my entire being.
I take in the love, peace and clairvoyance,

And they outpour freely
As I reach out with open arms

OPEN YOUR HEART

Open your heart
Let it roar
Open your heart
To the world within
Deep breath in
Open your heart

Become willing to explore
And accept the emotions that arise
Raw, fearless and vulnerable
Invite love in
Let abundance gush throughout
Blessings, wonders,
Mind expanding promises,
Your full soul expression

All reside in your heart

Trust what you hear there

Dancing stars and
Bubbling alchemy
In your open heart

NOUVELLE LUNE

from the shadow
I acknowledge what needs to go

I purge the stored encumbering heaviness
I untangle my own mess
and I call for it to be transmuted

from the new space created
a vast realm of envisioned possibilities
I give a voice to my sensibilities
writing them into being manifested

may this new moon bear the fruits
of fresh beginnings now in pursuit

We cannot live in a world interpreted for us by others. An interpreted world is not a hope. Part of the terror is to take back our listening, to use our own voice, to see our own light.

—Hildegard of Bingen

YOUR VOICE

Your voice comes from deep within.
It may shake and crumble,
It may have to fight the doubts and diminishments from
outside forces encounters.

Your voice may be loud and asserted,
Yet no one can hear it.

You may mistake your voice with ego fears
Arising in your head, perceived in your ears.

But your true voice is sturdy and stable,
Like the buried roots of a tree's stern foundation.
When your voice rises up ready to be shared,
You can be sure it won't tremble.

When you will let it come out of shyness and shrinkage,
It will roar,
You will roar,
Your soul will be so joyful
That you will be swept off your feet,
And fly on cloud nine.

What does your voice have to say?

She remembered who she was and the game changed.

—Laliah Deliah

PERMISSION

Only you can give it to yourself.
Only you can withhold it.
It's not about deserving or being good enough.
It's about recognising your influence over your entire life.
The permission is already yours.

Give yourself permission
To walk away
To sleep in
To nix
To not respond right away.

Give yourself permission
To investigate whatever is poking your awareness
To pause
To linger in the breath
To change your mind.

Give yourself permission
To let go
To be happy
To do what you've never done before
To give yourself what you need.

Give yourself permission
To tell yourself the truth
To listen to your intuition
To do what brings you joy
To put yourself first.

Give yourself permission
To stop playing small
And to dream big
To be all that you are
And embody your potential.

Start there. Give yourself permission.

A DIRECT LINE TO GOD

An inhale.
Presence.
An exhale.
Inner smile.

I am home.

YOU DESERVE THE BEST

You deserve to be happy
And to feel glee in everything you do

You deserve peace of mind
And down time

You deserve to put yourself first
And to let yourself be nursed

You deserve to love limitlessly
And to be loved like royalty

You deserve luxury
And positivity

You deserve all the sparkles in the world
And to adorn yourself with pearls

You deserve to trust yourself
And to feel safe

You deserve space
And to move without a trace

You deserve soft and *hygge* textures
You deserve gold glitter gestures

You deserve to treat your body with respect
And free yourself up when not perfect

You deserve to take all the time you need
Oh darling, go slow indeed

You deserve abundance
And expensive wines

You deserve to expand and glow
Unafraid of what may grow

Yes, you, beautiful friend,
You deserve the best

The only journey is the one within.

—Rainer Maria Rilke

LOOKING INWARDS

Opening the window onto my inwardness
Leaving fears and doubts at the door
Stepping intimately into the house of my Self
Exploring like a curious wanderer
Following the breath as my guide
I go deep
Deep within

While the back expands, the front folds
The rhythm of my breath like waves arising and dissolving
Unhurried, reposeful breath
Like the quieting melody of a lullaby
Meandering around my internal geography
A snowy mountain
A misty meadow
A barren tundra
A noisy waterfall
A thick forest
A lush garden
A tranquil lake

There is no striving or achieving
Only maundering in the rich inmost landscape
There is no doing or trying
Only breathing

Only being
Remarkably freeing

I found a corner of my heart that had been left unturned
I found home in that corner of my heart

And to make an end is to make a beginning. The end is where we start from.

— T.S. Eliot

CATERPILLAR

Nature awakening
From hibernation to spring
Leaving behind the cold dormant soil
And making place for the burgeons
Not quite sure of where we are going but proceeding anyway

Transition
From caterpillar to butterfly
Every cell of our being calling for growth and transformation
Consciousness expanding
Vibrations rising
Heart awakening
Strength renewing

Metamorphosis
We surrender and let it flow,
No forcing, no pushing,
No wishing it to be any different from what it is morphing
into
Moving slowly, with every breath, unhurriedly
Being present
Open to the journey
Of the revolution of our spirit

Let it happen
Support it, receive it
Enjoy it, embrace it
Your rebirth, your transformation, your evolution

It is through the body that everything comes through the mind. It is through and with your body that you have to reach realization of being a spark of divinity. How can we neglect the temple of the spirit?

—B.K.S. Iyengar

IT IS THROUGH THE BODY THAT EVERYTHING COMES TO THE MIND

Come into the temple of your own being.
Your body hosting your mind and enabling you to move.
Your heart as sacred impulse of energy and sparkle of life.
Your soul as the chief.
Your inner compass as guidance.

Cultivate the connection with your interior geography,
As that internal sense always knows the way.
Your intuitiveness is your soul whispering to you,
Through your guts and heart, which are your two other brains.

Intuition must be set in motion; you need to invite it in.
Then, create the conditions to receive it and above all,
Trust its murmurs.
When you are clear on what you want,
The way is shown and the resources are provided.

Are you ready to get onto the road of your destiny, and to open the door of your visceral knowing?
Are you ready to listen?

SPRING EQUINOX PRAYER

May you find peace in being you
May you feel contentment inhabit your existence
May wisdom flourish in your mind
May wonder take over your soul
May your heart expand like petals unfolding
May you reunite with your sacred calling
May you honour the significant rebirth occurring within you
May you allow your deepest Self to emerge and rise
May your essence infuse your life with happiness and
miracles

Do you pay regular visits to yourself?

—Rumi

RESET

Unsettled
Doubtful
Agitated
Disquieted
Looking for a sign

Shake it
Centre
Recalibrate

Take a breath
Turn within
Trust yourself
Your hunches
And your urges

Another breath
Internal space
Calm sea
Bright star
Guiding moon

Your inner knowing
Loud and clear

Insist on yourself; never imitate. Your own gift you can present every moment with the cumulative force of a whole life's cultivation; but of the adopted talent of another, you have only an extemporaneous, half possession. That which each can do best, none but his Maker can teach him.

—Ralph Waldo Emerson

EN ROUTE TO SELF

On the road to Self,
you might doubt,
you might cry,
you will get lost,
and discouraged.

On the road to Self,
you will be tempted by external detours,
the ones that look easy, distracting
And are in fact misleading
But if your quest is pure,

On the road to Self,
you will discover unsuspected strength and drive,
you will uncover your limitless potential,
you will cultivate trust and faith in your heart,
you will realise the freedom of your art.

On the road to Self,
Should you look within
with kindness and goodwill,
you will access your own answers
and find the beatitude you never thought you could gather.

BALASANA (CHILD'S POSE)

Oh, sweet child!

Come home
Safe, within exiled
Like it all began
Curled up
Cradled
Warm

Head resting
Fists unclenching
Give in to the cushioning
Land softly
Breathe gently
Nurtured
Snugged
Revel in the lusciousness
Liberated from expectations
Linger with the sensations
Gradually melting
And shortly sound asleep

Wanting less feel like getting more.

—Tanya Arteburn

LESS IS MORE

Whether it is in our daily life, behaviour, approaches or asana practice, let us invite:

Less pushing and more allowing
less doing and more being
less holding and more loosening
less straining and more mellowing
less stretching and more breathing
less trying to be something that we are not, and just move to
the beat of our own heart
less talking and more listening
less eating and more chewing
less tensing more releasing
less worrying, and more trusting
less judging and more loving
less striving and more unwinding
less expecting something different and more embracing
what's already present
less resentment and more boundaries
less noise and more silence
less outer chaos and more inner peace
less is more.

Ease and simplicity.
Ease and simplicity.

UNFETTERED

Open yourself up
Reveal your heart
One petal at a time, like a lotus.

Enable your gifts to surface
Bloom and flourish in your fortress
Have faith in the process

Trust your journey
Slowly, patiently growing,
Rising into your power
Unashamedly
Unrestrained
Unconstrained

Embody your *dharma*
To the fullest
With your mighty heart and soul
Aligned
Stable
Cheerful

Determined to keep on expanding
Indifferent to extrinsic impressions
Remain rooted in your inherent wisdom

Live gracefully in harmony with the song of your soul,
Honouring your heart vibrations

AT HOME WITHIN

Open the door
Onto the path
That will lead you home

Step out of the frame
To explore the other side of the fence
And only find out
That the grass is not greener
Elsewhere

Get out of the frame
Out of the life
Out of the boundaries
That you believe contain and restrain you

To only realise that you fence yourself in
That your thoughts
Your beliefs
Your judgements are scaling you down

Merge your inner and outer worlds
To walk fiercely
The path that was there all along
Only waiting to take you home
Home to Self
At home within

POEMS *for* SOULFUL LIVING

Wherever you go, there you are.

—Jon Kabat Zinn

INTERNAL REVOLUTION

In this moment of stillness and contemplation
There is something whispering to me
In the fasting from language and movement
I am touching upon the sacred
It can be felt
In my inner sanctuary
There, in complete surrender
I receive the breath
Its magic and healing
There, in open and kind presence
Is our doorway to accessing our own wisdom

I want to be with those who know secret things or else alone.

—Rainer Maria Rilke

BUILD A HEART CULTURE

In a society that constantly pushes us to:
do more
achieve more
buy more
consume more
compete more
have more
spend more
hate more
divide more
fear more
look outside of ourselves,
And give our strength away,

It is of the utmost importance, even an act of rebellion that we:
pause more,
say no more,
take time out more,
slow down more,
breathe more,
sleep more,
be more,
recycle more,
support each other more,
love more.

Let's love ourselves more.
Love others more.
Nurture more.
Accept ourselves more.
Honour our needs more.
Follow our heart more.
Look within more.
Know ourselves more.
Reclaim our leadership more.
Cultivate compassion more.
Open our mind more.
Swap ignorance for wisdom.
Protect our Earth more.
Spread kindness more.
Build a heart culture more.

Build. A heart. Culture.

When it is dark enough, you can see the stars.

—Persian proverb

I GOT LOST

I got lost a while ago.
I let myself be carried by rive Life
with nowhere to go.

I trusted in the unseen force above me
to take me wherever I needed to be
in order to live and grow.

Spells and prayers,
Hope and faith,
Affirmations and manifestations
are not enough for the life travellers
and the truth seekers.

I got lost
and understood that being my Self
and part of the sisterhood
required vision and action.

Blending a bit of me and of the Oneness
to create the goodness
that is being shared with the brotherhood
is necessary
for balance and harmony.

DAYDREAMING

Daydreaming should be on our self-care list.
A daily practice. A ritual.

The mind can wander and go walkabout freely.
A short trip to another place
Without restrictions of time or space.

A floating and unbounded journey
To think beyond, to envision, to be inspired.

In the daydreaming zone, your innate knowledge and
wisdom come through louder.
Have you noticed?

Ah, the sweetness of wandering aimlessly.
Drifting through the day,
Indolently.

The creations of my imagination
Open and untethered.
Vast and sovereign.

The freedom of my mind
To travel here, there, everywhere.

Our deepest fear is not that we are inadequate. Our deepest fear is that we are powerful beyond measure. It is our light, not our darkness, that most frightens us. We ask ourselves, Who am I to be brilliant, gorgeous, talented, fabulous? Actually, who are you not to be? You are a child of God. Your playing small doesn't serve the world.

—Marianne Williamson

SHE

She, who worries and stays up at night
She, who stops herself from liberated expression
She, who is afraid of disappointing others or not being liked
She, who doesn't speak her own words to avoid confrontation
or maybe expansion
She, who thinks keeping things undercover will not stir
anything
She, who does her best to please others while forgetting her
own appeal
She, who gave up before even trying
She, who doubted herself so deeply it became almost real

I want to talk to her

She, who wakes up in the morning hankering after big
dreams
She, who makes the effort to take tiny steps everyday
She, who has lots to say, write or paint
She, who feels overwhelmed by how potent she can truly be

I want to tell her

Claim your right to be here
Befriend your inner critic
Call onto your younger self

Own your radiance
Take up space
Share what you need to say,
Even if you think it is too abstruse for mankind

Honour her,
She, who came here to live in full authenticity.

Tension is who you think you should be. Relaxation is who you are.

—Chinese proverb

SAVASANA

I exhale and let myself be held
Cradled in the arms of Earth Mother
I rest

Bare and unburdened
Grounded yet weightless
I float on river Life

In complete surrender
I watch myself breathing
Nothing else matters now

Rest
Peace
Stillness

I have yielded my body
Muscles and bones
And relinquished all remaining efforts
So that my heart and soul can abide in repose

Tranquil and spacious

A little death
Serene and attuned
A rebirth

Today, I dare to sit in silence and surrender to the quiet voice within.
Today, I promise to dance with my soul and to love the skin I am in.
Today I dare to breathe and see the beauty within it all.

—Ntathu Allen

WHEN THE NOISE FINALLY RECEDES AND QUIETENS

You will finally hear the sweet sound of your calling,
The heartbeat of the earth,
The vibrations of the trees
And the birdsong's soulful melody.

Hitch your wagon to a star.

—Ralph Waldo Emerson

BECAUSE YOUR LIGHT,

Your divinity,
Your prowess,
Your strength,
Your intuition,
Your truth,
Your essence,
Your power,
Your wisdom
Are residing deep within your heart,
Longing to be trusted,
Revealed
And expressed.

This is why we came here for.

END OF YEAR BLESSING

May you leave behind any tension and heaviness in your
heart
May you untether yourself from false identities and burdens
May you release anything that is not a true reflection of who
you are

May you shed the heavy coat disguising your true self,
Weighing you down and away from purpose

May you receive the blessing of clarity and courage
May you answer the resounding call of your soul

May you rise with boldness,
Strength and determination,
Demanding better for yourself

May you start the new year with purity of heart,
Truth in words
And precision in mind

May you bask into your essence
And stand fully into your light

Be the fortitude,
Vehemently or quietly,
Who grow and ascend

Without any doubt or fear
Despite chatter and obstacles

The one who feels and knows deep into her heart
That her dreams and visions are feasible
Waiting for you to invite them in
Heart wide open

CLOSING PRAYER

May you answer the call of your soul
The call to rise
To voice your truth
To walk forward courageously
With only love and wisdom in your heart
To live without regrets
And to be shining fully
The radiance of your being

ACKNOWLEDGEMENTS

To my Yoga students for your presence over the years and for your willingness to go within.

To my life partner who always knows how to find the words to encourage and support me. Thank you for your way of loving me.

To my son who makes me want to be brave and live to the best of my abilities.

To the teachers in my life who passed on their knowledge, wisdom and experience, and to those who didn't even know they were teaching me.

To my friend and Female Business Guide, Lysa Black, for her love and guidance.

ABOUT THE AUTHOR

Nadege Laure is an experienced Yoga, Mindfulness Meditation Teacher and Personal Development Coach whose self-inquiry journey began as a teenager when she discovered Buddhist meditation. Her mother's passing at a young age reinforced her desire for truth and purpose. Traveling the world in quest for these answers to Life, ultimately led her to the most important journey of all: the journey within. Nadege is dedicated to gently guiding you to go inwards in order to deepen your self-awareness, uncover your true nature and embody your purpose with ease and joy.

If you enjoyed the poems and wish to go further, I invite you to explore these offerings:
nadegelaure.com/offerings
nadegelaure.com/shop

Printed in Australia
Ingram Content Group Australia Pty Ltd
AUHW020928031123
385989AU00002B/5